My First
KOREAN
Dictionary

English-Korean

Designed and edited by Maria Watson
Translated by Mihee Song

Hippocrene Books, Inc.
New York

My First Korean Dictionary

English-Korean

Hippocrene Books, Inc. edition, 2019

For information, address:
HIPPOCRENE BOOKS, INC.
171 Madison Avenue
New York, NY 10016
www.hippocrenebooks.com

ISBN: 978-0-7818-1394-5

© Publishers

First edition, 2016

Published by arrangement with Biblio Bee Publications, an imprint of ibs Books (UK)
56, Langland Crescent, Stanmore HA7 1NG, U.K.

Printed at Star Print-O-Bind, New Delhi-110 020 (India)

Aa

actor

배우   bae-u

actress

여배우   yeo-bae-u

adult

어른   eo-reun

aeroplane
US English **airplane**

비행기
bi-haeng-gi

air conditioner

에어컨
e-eo-kheon

air hostess
US English **flight attendant**

비행기 여승무원
bi-haeng-gi yeo-seung-
mu-won

airport

공항   gong-hang

album

앨범   ael-beom

almond

아몬드   a-mon-deu

alphabet

알파벳   al-pha-bet

ambulance

응급차
eung-geub-cha

angel

천사   cheon-sa

animal

동물   dong-mul

ankle
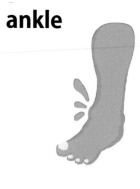
발목   bal-mok

ant

개미   gae-mi

antelope

영양   yeong-yang

antenna

안테나   an-te-na

apartment

아파트   a-pha-theu

ape
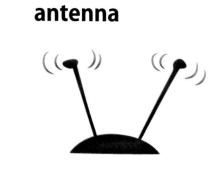
유인원   yu-in-won

apple
사과   sa-gwa

apricot

살구   sal-gu

apron

앞치마   aph-chi-ma

aquarium
수족관   su-jog-gwan

archery

양궁   yang-gung

architect

건축가
geon-chug-ga

arm

팔   phal

armour
US English **armor**

갑옷   gab-ot

arrow

화살   hwa-sal

artist

화가   hwa-ga

asparagus

아스파라거스
a-seu-pha-ra-geo-seu

astronaut

우주 비행사
u-ju   bi-haeng-sa

astronomer

천문학자
cheon-mun-hag-ja

athlete

육상선수
yuk-sang-seon-su

atlas

지도책   ji-do-chaek

aunt

이모, 고모, 아주머니
I-mo, Go-mo, A-ju-meoni

author

원작자
won-jag-ja

automobile

자동차
ja-dong-cha

autumn

가을　　　ga-eul

avalanche

눈사태　　nun-sa-the

award

상　　　　sang

axe

도끼　　　do-kki

baby

아기　　　a-gi

back

등　　　　deung

bacon

베이컨　　be-i-kheon

badge

배지　　　bae-ji

badminton

배드민턴
bae-deu-min-theon

bag

가방　　　ga-bang

baker

빵 굽는 사람
pang-gumneun-saa-ram

balcony

발코니　　bal-kho-ni

bald

대머리의
dae-meo-ri-ui

ball

공　　　　gong

ballerina

발레리나
bal-le-ri-na

balloon

풍선　　　phung-seon

bamboo

대나무　　dae-na-mu

banana

바나나　　ba-na-na

band

밴드　　　baen-deu

bandage

붕대　　　bung-dae

barbeque

바비큐　　ba-bi-khyu

a b c d e f g h i j k l m n o p q r s t u v w x y z

a
b
c
d
e
f
g
h
i
J
K
l
m
n
o
p
q
r
s
t
u
v
w
x
y
z

barn

헛간   heot-kan

barrel

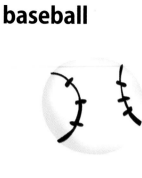

통   thong

baseball

야구   ya-gu

basket

바구니   ba-gu-ni

basketball

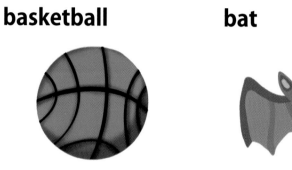

농구   nong-gu

bat

박쥐   bag-jwi

bath

목욕   mogyok

battery

배터리   bae-theo-ri

bay

만   man

beach

해변   hae-byeon

beak

부리   bu-ri

bean

콩   khong

bear

곰   gom

beard

턱수염
theok-su-yeom

bed

침대   chim-dae

bee

벌   beol

beetle

딱정벌레
ttak-jeong-beolle

beetroot

비트의 식용 뿌리
bi-theu-ui sig-yong-ppuri

bell

종   jong

belt

허리띠   heo-ri-tti

berry

베리   be-li

bicycle

자전거   ja-jeon-geo

billiards
US English **pool**

당구   dang-gu

bin

통, 저장통
tong, Jeo-jang-tong

a **b** c d e f g h i J k l m n o p q r s t u v w x y z

bird

새   say

biscuit

과자   gwa-ja

black

검은   geom-eun

blackboard

칠판   chil-phan

blanket

담요   dam-yo

blizzard

눈보라   nun-bo-ra

blood

피   phi

blue

파란   pha-ran

boat

배   bae

body

몸   mom

bone

뼈   ppyeo

book

책   chaek

boot

부츠   bu-cheu

bottle

병   byeong

bow

나비 넥타이
na-bi nek-thai

bowl

그릇   geu-reut

box

상자   sang-ja

boy

소년   son-yeon

bracelet

팔찌   phal-jji

brain
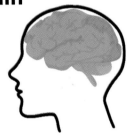
뇌   noe

branch

나뭇가지
na-mut-ga-ji

bread

빵   ppang

breakfast

아침 식사
a-chim sig-sa

brick

벽돌   byeog-dol

a b c d e f g h i j k l m n o p q r s t u v w x y z

a b c d e f g h i J k l m n o p q r s t u v w x y z

bride

신부　　　sin-bu

bridegroom

신랑　　　sin-lang

bridge

다리　　　da-ri

broom
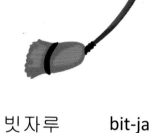
빗자루　　bit-ja-ru

brother

형, 오빠, 남동생
hyeong, oppa,
nam-dong-saeng

brown

갈색　　　gal-saek

brush

솔　　　　sol

bubble

거품　　geo-phum

bucket

들통　　　deul-thong

buffalo

물소　　　mul-so

building

건물　　　geon-mul

bulb

전구　　　jeon-gu

bull

황소　　hwang-so

bun

번빵　　beon-ppang

bunch

다발　　da-bal

bundle

꾸러미　　kku-reo-mi

bungalow

단층집
dan-cheung-jip

burger

버거　　beo-geo

bus

버스　　beo-seu

bush

관목　　gwan-mok

butcher

도살업자, 정육점 주인
do-sar-eop-ja,
jeong-yuk-jeom- ju-in

butter

버터　　beo-theo

butterfly

나비　　na-bi

button

단추　　dan-chu

Cc

cabbage

양배추
yang-bae-chu

cabinet

선반, 장
seon-ban, jang

cable

굵은 밧줄
gul-geun-ba-jjul

cable car

케이블 카
ke-i-beul kha

cactus

선인장   seo-nin-jang

cafe

카페   kha-phe

cage

새장   sae-jang

cake

케익   kheik

calculator

계산기   gye-san-gi

calendar

달력   dal-lyeok

calf

송아지   song-a-ji

camel

낙타   nag-tha

camera

카메라   kha-me-ra

camp

야영지   ya-yeong-ji

can

깡통   kkang-thong

canal

운하   un-ha

candle

양초   yang-cho

canoe

카누   kha-nu

canteen

구내식당
gu-nae-sig-dang

cap

모자   mo-ja

captain

선장   seon-jang

car

자동차
ja-dong-cha

caravan

이동식 주택
i-dong-sik ju-thaek

card

카드   kha-deu

carnival

축제   chug-je

carpenter

목수   mog-su

carpet

카펫   kha-phet

carrot

당근   dang-geun

cart
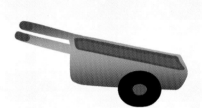
수레   su-re

cartoon

만화   man-hwa

cascade

작은 폭포
jag-eun phog-pho

castle

성   seong

cat

고양이   go-yang-I

caterpillar

애벌레
ae-beol-le

cauliflower

꽃양배추
kkoch-yang-bae-chu

cave

동굴   dong-gul

ceiling

천장   cheon-jang

centipede

지네   ji-ne

centre
US English **center**

중심   jung-sim

cereal

곡류   gog-ryu

chain

사슬   sa-seul

chair

의자   ui-ja

chalk

백악, 분필
bae-gak, bun-phil

cheek

뺨   ppyam

cheese

치즈   chi-jeu

chef

요리사   yo-ri-sa

cherry

버찌   beo-jji

chess

체스　　che-seu

chest

가슴　　ga-seum

chick

병아리　byeong-a-ri

chilli
US English **chili**

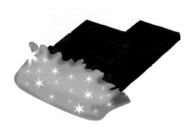

고추　　go-chu

chimney

굴뚝　　gul-ttuk

chin

턱　　　theok

chocolate

초콜릿
cho-khol-lit

christmas

크리스마스
keu-ri-seu-ma-seu

church

교회　　gyo-hoe

cinema

영화관
yeong-hwa-gwan

circle

원형
won-hyeong

circus

곡예단
gog-ye-dan

city

도시　　　do-si

classroom

교실　　　gyo-sil

clinic

병원　　byeong-won

clock

시계　　　si-gye

cloth

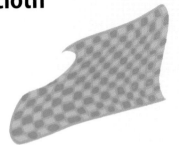

옷감　　　ot-gam

cloud

구름　　　gu-reum

clown

광대　　gwang-dae

coal

석탄　　seog-than

coast

해안　　　hae-an

coat

외투　　　oe-thu

cobra

코브라　kho-beu-ra

cockerel
US English **rooster**

어린 수탉

eo-rin　su-tha-lk

19

cockroach

바퀴벌레
ba-khwi-beol-le

coconut

코코넛
kho-kho-neot

coffee

커피   kheo-phi

coin

동전   dong-jeon

colour
US English **color**

색   saek

comb

빗   bit

comet

혜성   hye-seong

compass

나침반
na-chim-ban

computer

컴퓨터
kheom-phyu-theo

cone

원뿔   won-ppul

container

용기   yong-gi

cook

요리하다
yo-ri-ha-dak

cookie

과자　　　　　gwa-ja

cord

끈, 코드
kkeun, khod

corn

옥수수　　　ok-su-su

cot

간이 침대
gan-i　chim-dae

cottage

작은 집　jag-eun　jib

cotton

목화　　　　mog-hwa

country

나라　　　　　na-ra

couple

한 쌍, 부부
han-ssang, bu-bu

court

법정　　　beob-jeong

cow

암소　　　　am-so

crab

게　　　　　　　ge

crane

기중기　　gi-jung-gi

crayon

크레용
kheu-re-yong

crocodile

악어 　　　ag-eo

cross

십자가 　　sib-ja-ga

crow

까마귀 　kka-ma-gwi

crowd

군중 　　　gun-jung

crown

왕관 　　wang-gwan

cube

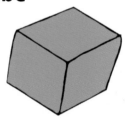

정육면체
jeong-yug-myeon-che

cucumber

오이 　　　　　oi

cup

잔 　　　　　jan

cupboard

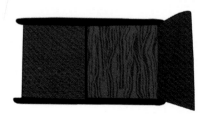

찬장 　　chan-jang

curtain

커튼 　kheo-theun

cushion

쿠션 　khu-syeon

Dd

dam

댐　　　　da-em

dancer

춤 추는 사람
chum-chu-neun-sa-ram

dart

다트　　　da-teu

data

자료　　　ja-ryo

dates

대추　　　dae-chu

daughter

딸　　　　ttal

day

날　　　　nal

deck

카드의 한 벌
kha-deu-han-beol

deer

사슴　　　sa-seum

den

굴　　　　gul

dentist

치과 의사
chi-gwa ui-sa

desert

사막　　　sa-mak

design

디자인　　　di-ja-in

desk

책상　　　chaeg-sang

dessert

후식　　　hu-sik

detective

형사　　　hyeong-sa

diamond

금강석
geum-gang-seok

diary

일기　　　il-gi

dice

주사위　　　ju-sa-wi

dictionary

사전　　　sa-jeon

dinosaur

공룡　　　gong-ryong

disc

원반, 레코드
won-ban, re-kho-d

dish

접시　　　jeob-si

diver

잠수부   jam-su-bu

dock

부두   bu-du

doctor

의사   ui-sa

dog

개   gae

doll

인형   in-hyeong

dolphin

돌고래   dol-go-rae

dome

돔   dom

domino

도미노   do-mi-no

donkey

당나귀
dang-na-gwi

donut

밀가루 반죽 덩어리
mil-ga-ru-ban-juk-
deong-eo-ri

door

문   mun

dough

도우   do-u

a b c **d** e f g h i J k l m n o p q r s t u v w x y z

dragon

용   yong

drain

배수하다
bae-su-hada

drawer

서랍   seo-rab

drawing

그림   geu-rim

dream

꿈   kkum

dress

옷   ot

drink

음료   eum-ryo

driver

운전자   un-jeon-ja

drop

물방울   mul-bang-ul

drought

가뭄   ga-mum

drum

북   buk

duck

오리   o-ri

dustbin
US English **trash can**

쓰레기통
sseu-re-gi-thong

duvet

이불　　　i-bul

dwarf

난쟁이　　nan-jaeng-i

Ee

eagle

독수리　　dog-su-ri

ear

귀　　　　gwi

earring

귀걸이　　gwi-geo-ri

earth

지구　　　ji-gu

earthquake

지진　　　ji-jin

earthworm

지렁이　　ji-reong-i

eclipse

식　　　　sik

edge

가장자리
ga-jang-jari

a
b
c
d
e
f
g
h
i
j
k
l
m
n
o
p
q
r
s
t
u
v
w
x
y
z

eel

장어　　　jang-eo

egg

알　　　al

eight

여덟　　　yeo-deolp

elastic

고무줄　　　go-mu-jul

elbow

팔꿈치
phal-kkum-chi

electrician

전기 기사
jeon-gi　gi-sa

electricity

전기　　　jeon-gi

elephant

코끼리　　　kho-kki-ri

elevator

엘리베이터
ell-i-be-i-theo

elf

요정　　　yo-jeong

email

이메일　　　i-me-il

embroidery

자수　　　ja-su

engine

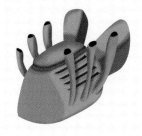

엔진　　　en-jin

entrance

입구　　　ib-gu

envelope

봉투　　　bong-thu

equator

적도　　　jeog-do

equipment

장비　　　jang-bi

eraser

고무지우개
go-mu-ji-u-gae

escalator

에스컬레이터
e-seu-kheol-le-i-theo

eskimo

에스키모
e-seu-khi-mo

evening

저녁　　　jeo-nyeok

exhibition

전시회　　jeon-si-hoe

eye

눈　　　nun

eyebrow

눈썹　　　nun-sseop

Ff

fabric

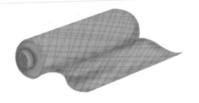

직물　　jig-mul

face

얼굴　　eol-gul

factory

공장　　gong-jang

fairy

요정　　yo-jeong

family

가족　　ga-jog

fan

선풍기
seon-phung-gi

farm

농장　　nong-jang

farmer

농부　　nong-bu

fat

뚱뚱한
ttung-ttung-han

father

아버지　　a-beo-ji

feather

깃털　　git-theol

female

여성   yeo-seong

fence

울타리   ul-tha-ri

ferry

여객선
yeo-gaeg-seon

field

들판   deul-phan

fig

무화과
mu-hwa-gwa

file

서류철
seo-ryu-cheol

film

영화   yeong-hwa

finger

손가락   son-ga-rak

fire

불   bul

fire engine

소방차
so-bang-cha

fire fighter

소방수
so-bang-su

fireworks

불꽃   bul-kkot

a b c d e f g h i j k l m n o p q r s t u v w x y z

fish

생선　　saeng-seon

fist

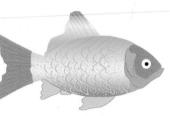

주먹　　ju-meok

five

다섯　　da-seot

flag

국기　　guk-gi

flame

불길　　bul-gil

flamingo

홍학　　hong-hak

flask

플라스크
pheul-la-seu-kheu

flock

떼, 무리　　tte, mu-ri

flood

홍수　　hong-su

floor

바닥　　ba-dak

florist

꽃가게 주인
kkot-kagye-ju-yin

flour

밀가루　　mil-ga-ru

flower

꽃   kkot

flute

플루트
pheul-lu-theu

fly

날다   nal-da

foam

거품   geo-phum

fog

안개   an-gae

foil

포일   pho-il

food

음식   eum-sik

foot

발   bal

football
US English **soccer**

축구   chug-gu

forearm

팔뚝   phal-ttuk

forehead

이마   i-ma

forest

삼림   sam-rim

fork

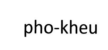

포크   pho-kheu

fortress

요새   yo-sae

fountain

분수   bun-su

four

넷   net

fox

여우   yeo-u

frame

액자   aeg-ja

freezer

냉동고
naeng-dong-go

fridge
US English **refrigerator**

냉장고
naeng-jang-go

friend

친구   chin-gu

frog

개구리   gae-gu-ri

fruit

과일   gwa-il

fumes

매연   mae-yeon

funnel

깔때기
kkal-ttae-gi

furnace

아궁이, 화덕, 용광로
a-gung-i, hwa-deok,
yong-gwang-no

furniture

가구   ga-gu

Gg

gadget

도구   do-gu

gallery

미술관
mi-sul-gwan

game

경기   gyeong-gi

gap

간격, 틈
gan-gyeok, theum

garage

차고   cha-go

garbage

쓰레기   sseu-re-gi

garden

뜰   tteul

garland

화환   hwa-hwan

a b c d e **f** **g** h i j J k l m n o p q r s t u v w x y z

garlic

마늘 ma-neul

gas

기체 gi-che

gate

문 mun

gem

보석 bo-seok

generator

발전기
bal-jeon-gi

germ

미생물
mi-saeng-mul

geyser

간헐 온천
gan-heol on-cheon

ghost

유령 yu-ryeong

giant

거인 geo-in

gift

선물 seon-mul

ginger

생강 saeng-gang

giraffe

기린 gi-rin

girl

소녀 son-yeo

glacier

빙하 bing-ha

glass

유리 yu-ri

glider

글라이더
geul-la-i-deo

globe

지구본 ji-gu-bon

glove

장갑 jang-gap

glue

접착제
jeob-chag-je

goal

목표 mog-phyu

goat

염소 yeom-so

gold

금 geum

golf

골프 gol-pheu

goose

거위 geo-wi

a
b
c
d
e
f
g
h
i
J
k
l
m
n
o
p
q
r
s
t
u
v
w
x
y
z

gorilla

고릴라   go-ril-la

grain

곡물   gug-mul

grandfather

할아버지
hal-a-beo-ji

grandmother

할머니   halmeoni

grape

포도   pho-do

grapefruit

그레이프프루트
geu-le-i-pheu-pheu-ru-theu

grass

풀   phul

grasshopper

메뚜기   me-ttu-gi

gravel

자갈   ja-gal

green

녹색   nog-saek

grey

회색   hwe-saek

grill

그릴   geu-ril

grocery

식료품
sig-lyo-phum

ground

땅 ttang

guard

경비원
gyung-bi-won

guava

궈바 gwo-ba

guide

안내원 an-ne-won

guitar

기타 gi-ta

gulf

만 man

gun

총 chong

gypsy

집시 jib-si

Hh

hair

머리카락
meo-ri-kharak

hairbrush

솔빗 sol-bit

a
b
c
d
e
f
g
h
i
J
k
l
m
n
o
p
q
r
s
t
u
v
w
x
y
z

hairdresser

미용사
mi-yong-sa

half

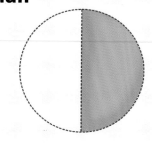

반   ban

hall

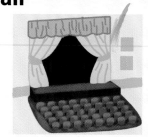

홀   hol

ham

햄   haem

hammer

망치   mang-chi

hammock

해먹   hae-meok

hand

손   son

handbag

손가방
son-ga-bang

handicraft

수공예
su-gong-ye

handkerchief

손수건
son-su-geon

handle

손잡이   sonjab-i

hanger

옷걸이   ot-geor-i

harbour
US English **harbor**

항구   hang-gu

hare

토끼   to-kki

harvest

수확   su-hwak

hat

모자   mo-ja

hawk

매   mae

hay

건초   geon-cho

head

머리   meo-ri

headphone

헤드폰
he-d-phon

heap

무더기
mu-deo-gi

heart

심장   sim-jang

heater

난방기
nan-bang-gi

hedge

산울타리, 헤지
san-ul-tha-ri, he-ji

heel
뒤꿈치, 굽
dwi-kkum-chi, gup

helicopter
헬리콥터
hel-li-khob-theo

helmet
헬멧   hel-met

hen
암탉   am-thalk

herb
약초   yag-cho

herd
떼, 무리(소, 양)
tte, mu-ri (so, yang)

hermit
은둔자   eun-dun-ja

hill
언덕   eon-deok

hippopotamus
하마   ha-ma

hive
벌집   beol-jip

hole
구덩이   gu-deong-i

honey
꿀   kkul

hood
두건, 후드
du-keon, hu-d

hook
걸이   geo-ri

horn
뿔   ppul

horse
말   mal

hose
호스   ho-seu

hospital
병원
byeong-won

hotdog
핫도그
has-do-geu

hotel
호텔   ho-thel

hour
시간   si-gan

house
집   jib

human
인간   in-gan

hunter
사냥꾼
san-yang-kkun

hurricane

허리케인
heo-ri-khe-in

husband

남편
nam-phyeon

hut

o-du-mak

오두막

Ii

ice

eor-eum

얼음

iceberg

bing-san

빙산

ice cream

아이스크림
a-i-seu-kheu-rim

idol

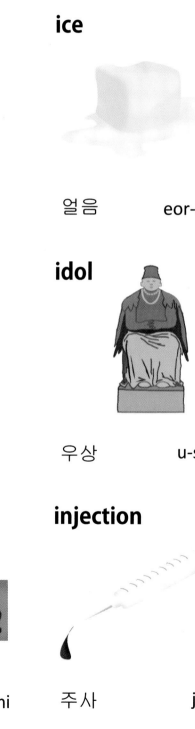

우상   u-sang

igloo

이글루   i-geul-lu

inch

인치   in-chi

injection

주사   ju-sa

injury

부상   bu-sang

ink

잉크   ing-kheu

inn

여관   yeo-gwan

insect
곤충   gon-chung

inspector

조사관
jo-sa-gwan

instrument

악기   ag-gi

internet
인터넷   in-theo-net

intestine
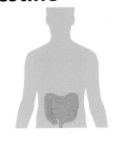
장   jang

inventor

창안자
chang-an-ja

invitation

초대   cho-dae

iron

다리미   da-ri-mi

island

섬   seom

ivory

상아   sang-a

Jj

jackal

자칼　　ja-khal

jacket

재킷　　jae-khit

jackfruit

잭푸르트
jaeg-phu-reu-theu

jam

잼　　jaem

jar

항아리, 단지
han-ga-ri, dan-ji

javelin

투창　　thu-chang

jaw

턱　　theok

jeans

바지　　ba-ji

jelly

젤리　　jel-li

jetty

둑　　duk

jewellery
US English **jewelry**

보석류
bo-seog-nyu

jigsaw

조각그림
jo-gag-geu-rim

jockey

기수　　　　gi-su

joker

농담하는 사람
nong-dam ha-neun sa-ram

journey

여행　　yeo-haeng

jug

주전자, 항아리
ju-jeon-ja, han-ga-ri

juggler

저글링하는 사람
jeo-geul-ling ha-neun
sa-ram

juice

주스　　　ju-seu

jungle

밀림　　　mil-lim

jute

황마　　　hwang-ma

Kk

kangaroo

캥거루
khaeng-geo-ru

kennel

개집　　　gae-jip

kerb
US English **curb**

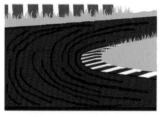

연석   yeon-seok

kerosene

등유   deung-yu

ketchup

케첩   khe-cheop

kettle

주전자   ju-jeon-ja

key

열쇠   yeol-soe

keyboard

키보드
khi-bo-deu

key ring

열쇠 고리
yeol-soe gori

kidney

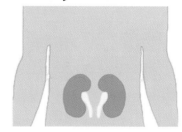

신장   sin-jang

kilogram

킬로그램
khil-lo-geu-raem

king

왕   wang

kiosk

오두막, 신문매점
o-du-mak, sin-mun-
mae-jeom

kiss

뽀뽀   ppo-ppo

kitchen

부엌   bu-eokh

kite

연   yeon

kitten

새끼 고양이
sae-kki go-yang-I

kiwi

키위   khi-wi

knee

무릎   mu-reuph

knife

칼   khal

knight

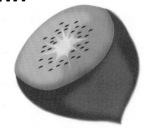

기사   gi-sa

knitwear

뜨개질 한 옷
tteo-gae-jil-han-ot

knob

손잡이   son-jab-I

knock

노크   no-kheu

knot

매듭
mae-deup

knuckle

손가락 관절
son-garak gwan-jeol

a b c d e f g h i j k l m n o p q r s t u v w x y z

Ll

label

상표　　　sang-phyo

laboratory

실험실
sil-heom-sil

lace

신발끈
sinbal-kkeun

ladder

사닥다리
sa-dag-da-ri

lady

여자　　　yeo-ja

ladybird
US English **ladybug**

무당벌레
mu-dang-beol-le

lagoon

초호　　　cho-ho

lake

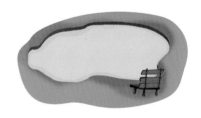

호수　　　ho-su

lamb

양　　　yang

lamp

등불　　deung-bbul

lamp post

가로등 기둥
ga-ro-deung gi-dung

land

땅　　　　　ttang

lane

길　　　　　gil

lantern

손전등
son-jeon-deung

laser

레이저　　　le-i-jeo

lasso

올가미밧줄
ol-ga-mi-bat-jul

latch

걸쇠　　　　geol-soe

laundry

세탁물
se-thag-mul

lawn

잔디밭
jan-di-bath

lawyer

변호사
byeon-ho-sa

layer
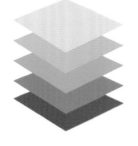
층　　　　　cheung

leaf

잎　　　　　iph

leather

가죽　　　　ga-juk

a
b
c
d
e
f
g
h
i
J
k
l
m
n
o
p
q
r
s
t
u
v
w
x
y
z

leg

다리   da-ri

lemon

레몬   le-mon

lemonade

레몬 탄산음료
le-mon than-san-eum-nyo

lens

렌즈   len-jeu

leopard

표범   phyo-beom

letter

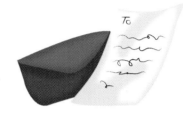

편지   phyeon-ji

letterbox
US English **mailbox**

우편함
u-phyeon-ham

lettuce

상추   sang-chu

library

도서관
do-seo-gwan

licence

DRIVER LICENCE
NYC23579081
FIRST NAME....jhsguyegyug
LAST NAME....jhwgdyugduwy
SEX............huhqi
HAIR............whuw
HT.............wihyu
WT.............uwguje
Expiry...........02-04-23
2/3/2014   62C FDRMN

면허   myeon-heo

lid

뚜껑   ttu-kkeong

light

빛   bit

lighthouse

등대　　　deung-dae

limb

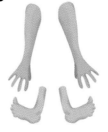

수족 손발
su-jok, son-bal

line

선　　　seon

lion

사자　　　sa-ja

lip

입술　　　ib-sul

lipstick

립스틱
lib-seu-thik

liquid

액체　　　aeg-che

list

목록　　　mog-nok

litre
US English **liter**

리터　　　ri-theo

living room

거실　　　geo-sil

lizard

도마뱀
do-ma-baem

load

부담량
bu-dam-nyang

a
b
c
d
e
f
g
h
i
J
K
l
m
n
o
p
q
r
s
t
u
v
w
x
y
z

a
b
c
d
e
f
g
h
i
J
k
l
m
n
o
p
q
r
s
t
u
v
w
x
y
z

loaf

덩어리
deong-eo-ri

lobster

바닷가재
ba-dat-ga-jae

lock

잠그다
jam-geu-da

loft

고미다락
go-mi-da-rak

log

통나무
thong-na-mu

loop

고리   go-ri

lorry

US English **truck**

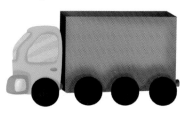

화물차
hwa-mul-cha

lotus

연꽃   yun-kkot

louse

이   i

luggage

짐   jim

lunch

점심   Jeom-sim

lung

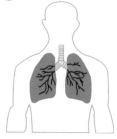

폐   phye

Mm

machine
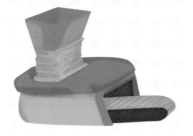
기계 gi-gye

magazine

잡지 jab-ji

magician

마술사
ma-sul-sa

magnet

자석 ja-seok

magpie

까치 kkachi

mail

우편 u-phyeon

mammal

포유동물
pho-yu-dong-mul

man

남자 nam-ja

mandolin

만돌린 man-dol-lin

mango

망고 man-go

map
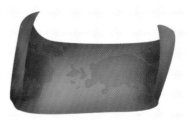
지도 ji-do

maple

단풍나무
dan-phung-na-mu

marble

대리석
dae-li-seok

market

시장　　　si-jang

mask

마스크
ma-seu-kheu

mast

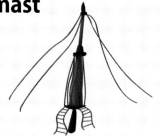

돛대　　　doch-dae

mat

매트　　　mae-theu

matchbox

성냥갑
seong-nyang-gap

mattress

매트리스
mae-theu-li-seu

meal

식사　　　Sik-sa

meat

고기　　　go-gi

mechanic

정비공
jeong-bi-gong

medicine

약, 의약　yak, ui-yak

melon

멜론   mel-lon

merchant

상인   sang-in

mermaid

인어   in-eo

metal
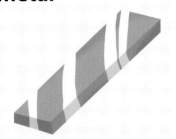
금속   geum-sok

metre
US English **meter**

미터   me-theo

microphone

마이크   ma-i-kheu

microwave

전자레인지
jeon-ja-re-in-ji

mile

마일   ma-il

milk

우유   u-yu

miner

광부   gwang-bu

mineral

광물   gwang-mul

mint
박하   bag-ha

minute
분   bun

mirror
거울   geo-ul

mobile phone
휴대폰
hyu-dae-phon

model
모델   mo-del

mole
두더지   du-deo-ji

money
돈   don

monk
수도자   sudo-ja

monkey
원숭이
won-sung-I

monster
괴물   goe-mul

month
달   dal

monument
기념물
gi-nyeom-mul

moon
달   dal

mop

대걸레
dae-geol-le

morning

아침　　a-chim

mosquito

모기　　mo-gi

moth

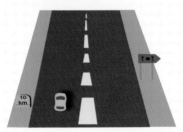

나방　　na-bang

mother

어머니　eo-meo-ni

motorcycle

오토바이
o-tho-ba-i

motorway

고속도로
go-sog-do-ro

mountain

산　　　san

mouse

쥐　　　jwi

mousetrap

쥐덫　　jwi-deoch

moustache

콧수염
khos-su-yeom

mouth

입　　　ip

mud

진흙   jin-heuk

muffin

머핀   meo-phin

mug

머그잔   meo-geu-jan

mule

노새   no-sae

muscle

근육   geun-yuk

museum

박물관
bag-mul-gwan

mushroom

버섯   beo-seot

music

음악   eu-mak

musician

음악가   eu-mak-ga

Nn

nail

못   mot

napkin

냅킨   naeb-khin

nappy
US English **diaper**

기저귀 gi-jeo-gwi

nature

자연 ja-yeon

neck

목 mok

necklace

목걸이 mok-geo-ri

necktie

넥타이 neg-thai

needle

바늘 ba-neul

neighbour
US English **neighbor**

이웃 iut

nest

둥지 dung-ji

net

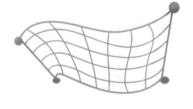

그물, 네트
geu-mul, net

newspaper

신문 sin-mun

night

밤 bam

nine

아홉 a-hop

a b c d e f g h i j k l m **n** o p q r s t u v w x y z

noodles

국수   gug-su

noon

정오   jeong-o

north
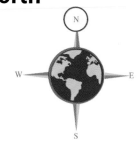
북   buk

nose
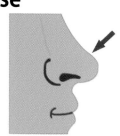
코   kho

note

메모   me-mo

notebook

공책   gong-chaek

notice

공고   gong-go

number

수   su

nun

수녀   su-nyeo

nurse

간호사   gan-ho-sa

nursery

탁아소   thag-a-so

nut

견과   gyeon-gwa

Oo

oar

노   no

observatory

관측소
gwan-cheug-so

ocean
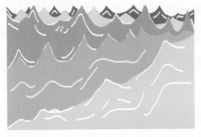
대양   dae-yang

octopus

문어   mun-eo

office

사무소   sa-mu-so

oil

석유   seog-yu

olive

올리브   ol-li-beu

omelette
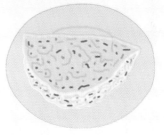
오믈렛   o-meul-let

one

일, 하나   il, hana

onion

양파   yang-pha

orange

오렌지   o-ren-ji

a b c d e f g h i j k l m n o p q r s t u v w x y z

orbit

궤도   gwe-do

orchard

과수원   gwa-su-won

orchestra

오케스트라
o-khe-seu-theu-ra

ostrich

타조   tha-jo

otter

수달   su-dal

oval

계란형
gye-ran-hyeong

oven

오븐   o-beun

owl

수리부엉이
su-ri-bu-eong-i

ox

황소   hwang-so

Pp

packet

한 묶음, 한 봉지
han-mu-kkum, han-bong-ji

page

쪽, 페이지
jjok, phe-i-ji

pain

아픔   a-pheum

paint

페인트   phe-in-theu

painting

그림   geu-rim

pair

한쌍   han-ssang

palace

궁전   gung-jeon

palm

손바닥   son-ba-dak

pan

냄비   naem-bi

pancake

팬케이크
phaen-khe-i-kheu

panda

팬더   phaen-deo

papaya

파파야   pha-pha-ya

paper

종이   jong-i

parachute

낙하산   nag-ha-san

a b c d e f g h i j k l m n o **p** q r s t u v w x y z

parcel

소포　　　so-pho

park

공원　　　gong-won

parrot

앵무새
aeng-mu-sae

passenger

승객　　　seung-gaek

pasta

파스타
pha-seu-tha

pastry

패스트리
phae-seu-theu-ri

pavement

보도　　　bo-do

paw

동물의 발
dong-mu-re-bal

pea

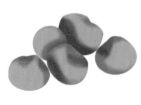

완두콩
wan-du-khong

peach

복숭아　　bog-sung-a

peacock

공작　　　gong-jak

peak

꼭대기　　kkok-dae-gi

peanut

땅콩   ttang-khong

pear

배   bae

pearl

진주   jin-ju

pedal

페달   phe-dal

pelican

펠리컨
phel-li-kheon

pen

펜   phen

pencil

연필   yeon-phil

penguin

펭귄   pheng-gwin

pepper

후추   hu-chu

perfume

향수   hyang-su

pet

애완동물
ae-wan-dong-mul

pharmacy

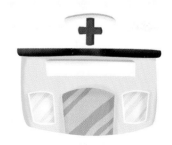

약국   yag-gug

a b c d e f g h i j k l m n o p q r s t u v w x y z

photograph

사진   sa-jin

piano

피아노   pi-a-no

picture

그림   geu-rim

pie

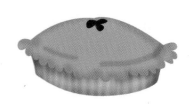

파이   pha-i

pig

돼지   dwae-ji

pigeon

비둘기   bi-dul-gi

pillar

기둥   gi-dung

pillow

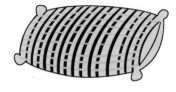

베개   be-gae

pilot

조종사   jo-jong-sa

pineapple

파인애플
pha-in-ae-pheul

pink

분홍색
bun-hong-saek

pipe

관   gwan

pizza

피자　　phi-ja

planet

행성　　haeng-seong

plant

식물　　sing-mul

plate

접시　　jeob-ssi

platform
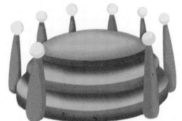
플랫폼
pheul-laet-phom

platypus

오리너구리
o-ri-neo-gu-ri

player

운동선수
un-dong-seon-su

plum

자두　　ja-du

plumber

배관공
bae-gwan-gong

plywood

합판　　hab-phan

pocket

호주머니
ho-ju-meo-ni

poet

시인　　si-in

a b c d e f g h i j k l m n o p q r s t u v w x y z

abcdefghiJklmnop qrstuvwxyz

polar bear

북극곰
buk-keuk-kom

police

경찰　　gyeong-chal

pollution

오염　　o-yeom

pomegranate

석류　　seog-nyu

pond

연못　　yeon-mot

porcupine

호저　　ho-jeo

port

항구　　hang-gu

porter

짐꾼　　jim-kkun

postcard

엽서　　yeob-seo

postman

우체부　　uche-bu

post office

우체국　　uche-guk

pot

화분　　hwa-bun

potato

감자   gam-ja

powder

가루   ga-ru

prawn
US English **shrimp**

새우   sae-u

priest

사제   sa-je

prince

왕자   wang-ja

prison

교도소   gyo-do-so

pudding

푸딩   pu-ding

pump

펌프   pheom-pheu

pumpkin

호박   ho-bak

puppet

꼭두각시
kkok-tu-kak-si

puppy

강아지   gang-a-ji

purse

지갑   ji-gap

a b c d e f g h i j k l m n o **p** q r s t u v w x y z

Qq

quail

메추라기
me-chu-ra-gi

quarry

채석장
chae-seog-jang

queen

여왕   yeo-wang

queue

줄   jul

quiver

화살통
hwa-sal-thong

Rr

rabbit

토끼   tho-kki

rack

선반   seon-ban

racket

라켓   ra-ket

radio

라디오   ra-di-o

radish

무   mu

raft
떼목   tten-mok

rain
비   bi

rainbow
무지개   mu-ji-gae

raisin
건포도
geon-pho-do

ramp
경사로   gyung-sa-ro

raspberry
산딸기
san-ttal-gi

rat
쥐   jwi

razor
면도기   myeon-do-gi

receipt
영수증
yeon-su-jeung

rectangle
직사각형
jig-sa-ga-khyeong

red
빨간   ppal-gaan

restaurant
식당   sik-ttang

rhinoceros

코뿔소 kho-ppul-so

rib

늑골 neug-gol

ribbon

리본 ri-bon

rice

밥 bap

ring

반지 ban-ji

river

강 gang

road

길 gil

robber

강도 gang-do

robe

예복 ye-bok

robot

로봇 ro-bot

rock

암석 am-seok

rocket

로켓 ro-ket

roller coaster

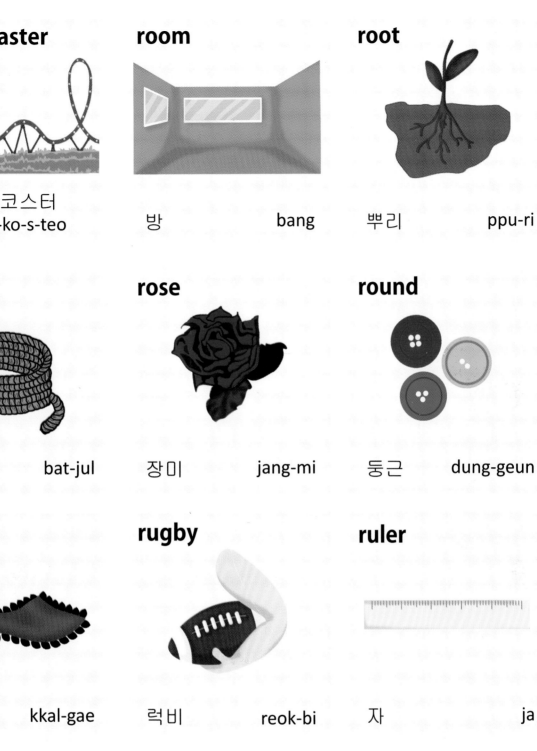

롤러코스터
ro-leo-ko-s-teo

room

방　　　　　bang

root

뿌리　　　　ppu-ri

rope

밧줄　　　　bat-jul

rose

장미　　　　jang-mi

round

둥근　　　　dung-geun

rug

깔개　　　　kkal-gae

rugby

럭비　　　　reok-bi

ruler

자　　　　　ja

Ss

sack

부대　　　　bu-dae

sail

항해, 돛
hang-hae, do-t

sailor

선원   seon-won

salad

샐러드
sael-leo-deu

salt

소금   so-geum

sand

모래   mo-rae

sandwich

샌드위치
saen-deu-wi-chi

satellite

위성   wi-seong

saucer

받침   bat-chim

sausage

소시지   so-si-ji

saw

톱   thop

scarf

목도리   mog-do-ri

school

학교   hak-kyo

scissors

가위   ga-wi

scooter

스쿠터
seu-khu-theo

scorpion

전갈　　jeon-gal

screw

나사　　na-sa

sea

바다　　ba-da

seal

물개　　mul-gae

seat

자리　　ja-ri

see-saw

시소　　si-so

seven

일곱　　il-gop

shadow
그림자　　geu-rim-ja

shampoo

샴푸　　syam-phu

shark

상어　　sang-eo

sheep

양　　yang

a b c d e f g h i j k l m n o p q r **s** t u v w x y z

shelf

선반   seon-ban

shell

조개 껍데기
jo-gae-kkeop-te-gi

shelter

주거지   ju-geo-ji

ship

배   bae

shirt

셔츠   syeo-cheu

shoe

신발   sin-bal

shorts

반바지   ban-ba-ji

shoulder

어깨   eo-kkae

shower

샤워   sha-weo

shutter

덧문   deon-mun

shuttlecock

셔틀콕
syeo-theul-khok

signal

신호   sin-ho

silver

은   eun

sink

세면대, 수채, 싱크대
se-myeon-dae, su-chae,
sinkh-dae

sister

언니; 누나
eon-ni; nu-na

six

여섯   yeo-seot

skate

스케이트   s-khet

skeleton

해골, 골격
hae-gol, gol-gyuk

ski

스키   seu-khi

skin

피부   phi-bu

skirt

스커트
seu-kheo-theu

skull

두개골   du-gae-gol

sky

하늘   ha-neul

skyscraper

고층 건물
go-cheung geon-mul

a b c d e f g h i j k l m n o p q r **s** t u v w x y z

slide

미끄럼틀
mi-kkeu-reom-theul

slipper

실내화　　　sil-ae-hwa

smoke

연기　　　yeon-gi

snail

달팽이
dal-phaeng-i

snake

뱀　　　baem

snow

눈　　　nun

soap

비누　　　bi-nu

sock

양말　　　yang-mal

sofa

소파　　　so-pha

soil

토양　　　tho-yang

soldier

군인　　　gun-in

soup

수프　　　su-pheu

space

우주   u-ju

spaghetti

스파게티
seu-pha-ge-thi

sphere

구   gu

spider

거미   geo-mi

spinach

시금치   si-geum-chi

sponge

스펀지   seu-peon-ji

spoon

숟가락   sut-ga-rak

spray

스프레이, 분무기
s-p-re-y, bun-mu-gi

spring

봄   bom

square

정사각형 모양의
jeong-sa-gag-hyeong
mo-yang-ui

squirrel

다람쥐
da-ram-jwi

stadium

경기장
gyeong-gi-jang

a
b
c
d
e
f
g
h
i
J
K
l
m
n
o
p
q
r
s
t
u
v
w
x
y
z

stairs

계단　　　gye-dan

stamp

우표　　　u-phyo

star

별　　　byeol

station

역　　　yeok

statue

조각상　　jo-gag-sang

stethoscope

청진기
cheong-jin-gi

stomach

배　　　bae

stone

돌　　　dol

storm

폭풍　　phog-phung

straw

빨대　　ppal-dae

strawberry

딸기　　ttal-gi

street

도로　　do-ro

student

학생   hag-saeng

submarine

잠수함
jam-su-ham

subway

지하철
ji-ha-cheol

sugar

설탕   seol-thang

sugarcane

사탕수수
sa-thang-su-su

summer

여름   yeo-reum

sun

해   hae

supermarket

슈퍼마켓
syu-pheo-ma-khet

swan

백조   baeg-jo

sweet

달콤한
dal-khom-han

swimming pool

수영장
su-yeong-jang

swimsuit

수영복
su-yeong-bok

a b c d e f g h i j k l m n o p q r **s** t u v w x y z

swing

그네 geu-ne

switch

스위치 seu-wi-chi

syrup

시럽 si-reop

table

식탁 sig-thak

tall

키가 큰
ki-ga-kheun

tank

탱크 thaeng-kheu

taxi

택시 thaeg-si

tea

차 cha

teacher

선생 seon-saeng

teeth

치아 chi-a

telephone

전화 jeon-hwa

television

텔레비전
thel-le-bi-jeon

ten

열　　　　　yeol

tennis

테니스　　　the-ni-seu

tent

천막　　　cheon-mak

thief

도둑　　　do-duk

thread

실　　　　　sil

three
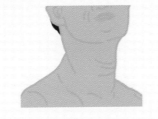
세　　　　　se

throat

목　　　　　mok

thumb

엄지손가락
eom-ji-son-ga-rak

ticket

표　　　　　phyo

tiger

호랑이　　ho-rang-I

toe
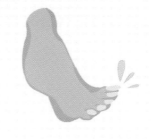
발가락　　bal-ga-rak

a b c d e f g h i j k l m n o p q r s **t** u v w x y z

tofu

두부　　du-bu

tomato

토마토
tho-ma-tho

tongue

혀　　hyeo

tool

도구　　dogu

toothbrush

칫솔　　chis-sol

toothpaste

치약　　chi-yak

tortoise

거북　　geo-buk

towel

수건　　su-geon

tower

탑　　thap

toy

장난감
jang-nan-gam

tractor

트랙터
theu-raeg-theo

train
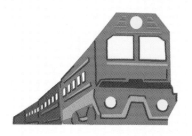
기차　　gi-cha

tree

나무   na-mo

triangle

삼각형
sam-gag-hyeong

tub

목욕통
mok-yok-thong

tunnel

터널   theo-neol

turnip

순무   sun-mu

tyre

US English **tire**

타이어   tha-i-eo

Uu

umbrella

우산   u-san

uncle

삼촌   sam-chon

uniform

제복   je-bok

university

대학   dae-hak

utensil

부엌 세간
bu-eok se-gan

Vv

vacuum cleaner

진공 청소기
jin-gong-cheong-so-gi

valley

계곡   gye-gok

van

밴   baen

vase

꽃병   kkoch-byeong

vault

금고   geum-go

vegetable

채소   chae-so

veil

베일   be-il

vet

수의사   su-eo-sa

village

마을   ma-eul

violet

보라색   bo-ra-saek

violin

바이올린   ba-i-ol-lin

volcano

화산   hwa-san

volleyball

배구   bae-gu

vulture

독수리   dog-su-ri

Ww

waist

허리   heo-ri

waitress

종업원
jong-eob-won

wall

담   dam

wallet

지갑   ji-gap

walnut

호두   ho-du

wand

마술사 지팡이, 지휘봉
ma-sul-sa ji-phangi,
ji-hwi-bong

wardrobe

옷장   ot-jang

warehouse

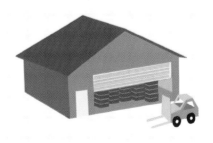

창고   chan-go

a b c d e f g h i j k l m n o p q r s t u v w x y z

wasp

말벌   mal-beol

watch

손목시계
son-mok-si-gye

water

물   mul

watermelon

수박   su-bak

web

거미줄   geo-mi-jul

whale

고래   go-rae

wheat

밀   mil

wheel

바퀴   ba-kwi

whistle

호각   ho-gak

white

하얀   hayan

wife

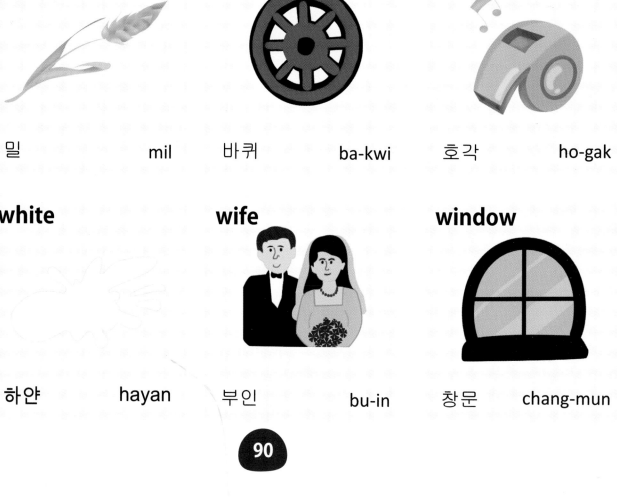

부인   bu-in

window

창문   chang-mun

wing

날개　　　nal-gae

winter

겨울　　　gyeo-ul

wizard

마법사　ma-beob-sa

wolf

늑대　　　neug-dae

woman

여자　　　yeo-ja

woodpecker

딱따구리
ttag-tta-gu-ri

wool

양털　　　yang-theol

workshop

작업장
jag-eob-jang

wrist

손목　　　son-mok

Xx

x-ray

엑스선　eg-seu-seon

xylophone

실로폰　sil-lo-phon

a b c d e f g h i J k l m n o p q r s t u v **w** **x** y z

Yy

yacht

요트 yo-theu

yak
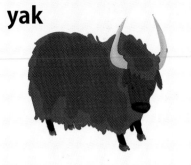
야크 ya-kheu

yard
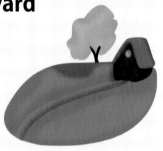
마당 mi-dang

yellow

노란 no-ran

yoghurt

요구르트
yo-gu-reu-theu

Zz

zebra

얼룩말 eol-lug-mal

zero

영 yeong

zip
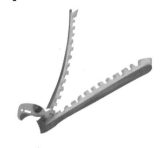
지퍼 ji-pheo

zodiac

황도대
hwang-do-dae

zoo

동물원
dong-mul-won